Learning about Rain

∞

Bill Freedman

FUTURECYCLE PRESS
www.futurecycle.org

Cover artwork, spider in rain storm, from the public domain; cover and interior book design by Diane Kistner; Chaparral Pro text and Bodoni Sans titling

Library of Congress Control Number: 2020934101

Published by FutureCycle Press
Athens, Georgia, USA

ISBN 978-1-942371-99-1

*It is with enduring love, admiration
and gratitude that I dedicate this collection
to my wife Helen and my children Jennifer and Etai.*

Contents

Four: Lapped Water

Five: Stone/Glass

One: Rain

Life

Keep Off The Grass,
it said,
the sign so low,
so overgrown,
I was two long strides
inside
before I saw it.
When I bent to read it,
a policeman, borderline obese
but supple,
tapped me on the shoulder,
reciting, fairly chanting as I rose,
"You remind me, if only
in its most predictable
and overrated aspect,
of the sun."
We spoke a while
of romance, dawdling,
family, retirement and travel
to the spotless cities of Japan.
"Another species,
so politely deferent
and repressed," he said,
"since '45," and I agreed.
He in the front seat, turning,
aware my audial receptors
were not the athletes they once were.
I in the back, handcuffed,
my voice muffled by a gallows hood,
but irrepressible, for the ages, breathing.

Tall Grass

They are never one.
As from a tribal or Oriental mother,
shoots, small replicas,
spring from their sides, reach up.

Wind has an easy time with tall grasses,
leans them into one another,
one into many as on a lurching subway car.
They do not complain.

When wind does this, even breezes,
their thinness knows it was intended.
Perhaps by the river that always moves.
Some say sky.

At the showering crest,
tiers of slender golden fingers,
skeletons of lost pitched rooves,
pagodas, tremble.

There is something distinctly Japanese
about them. Also the bowing,
even when all the rest is still,
the extravagant politeness.

Where they are tallest in another world,
a snake or leopard slithers through them undetected.
This, too, tall grass accepts as given,
makes a path for, uncomplaining, presses down.

When you walk through tall grasses,
they clutch at your ankles, as though they'd have you stay.
As though for all their stoic courage and acceptance,
there is something more familiar at the root.

Learning about Rain

Droplets fall on the spider's web,
each few seconds shake it.
From the look of her, nothing
in the hoary history of spiderhood
has prepared her, though it is rife with rain.

At each light or heavy touch, she skitters,
with Arachne's take on salivating gratitude
for all this luck, to the point of contact,
scarcely reaches when she is summoned back.
Now there, past noon,
now here, at 6 o'clock, and there again.
A family of flies delivered here or passing,
beehive struck and fallen in the wood,
a plague of locusts: spider lottery and jackpot,
all her own.

She scales her ladder, eagerly at first,
then slowly, hesitant, exhausted,
shrivels at the center
to a blackened bead, absorbs
the unforgiving buffeting of rain.
She knows, immersed too late,
she will leave no legacy, no message.
The young she thought to gorge
with all this wealth
will have to learn, in their own time,
about the rain.

Pre-Speech Guidelines for the Earth

"Thou, earth, thou, Speak" (*The Tempest*)

But be brief and mindfully selective.
Say nothing about stones.
We have felt them on our flesh and bones.
Half buried, on our faces, skulls.
We have heard enough.

Very little about trees.
A word or two on leaves as shrunken hands,
bark the fingerprints of lost volcanoes.
For the rest, what we need to know, we see,
and their roots run deep inside you.
They have leverage. You are too familiar.
What you reveal to one another we cannot hear.
We will suspect what you say.

Do not waste your voice on grass or flowers.
Nothing you explain
will be of vital interest or protect us.
We plant and pluck them,
trample and lie down among them.
They do not concern us.

We will have patience
for telling words about insects.
If you feel their weight when they crawl across you,
distinguish spiders, let us say, from beetles.
If you resent their burrowing
or welcome the intrusion,
the relief from boredom.

Time for revelations we can relate to,
about the ice and thaw,
about the thunder, lakes and rivers,
if they are meaningful to you.

If they touch your heart,
as they touch ours, if we admit them,
in ways we can scarcely imagine,
but would dwell upon if given hints.

It is these that fascinate and seize us,
that will hold our ears to your breastplate
for as long as you wish to speak.
Tell us, if you will, about the rain.

Pages

This book was forgotten once, left out in rain,
its pages stained and yeasty, like rheumatic wrists,
rugose, like the backs of old hands.

The poems on these pages are thoughtfully quiet.
They are about the natural world and its seasons.
But even the ones about the birds and blown leaves are quiet.

They might as well be only about snow.
Or about the new mother groping barefoot in the dark
of her infant's room for all she has lost, afraid to wake her.

Some are about love.
But even the ones about sorrow and separation whisper.
The pages are more truthful.

Especially about love.
When I turn them, louder when I try to straighten them,
like brittle bones they crack.

Stories

It's all right sometimes
to look at something
you know might be a poem.
The way rain funnels
from a cloud above the sea,
a coal chute, bordered, local.
One story out of many.
No resemblance to the one you're in,
the Ur myth,
return of the Second Day.
When it is raining,
there is rain; rain is.

Just to see it,
hand unmoving, mind at large.
Note equal swaths of clarity
on either side.
Imagine someone,
the gifted girl next door,
writing passionately about new love,
First Day, first light,
trusting you'll forever hold your piece
about the rain.

Weavers

Before the age of isolation,
spiders wove in covens.
Ten or twenty in a pleated room of corners.

Each spun a taut suspenseful tale.
Not of journeys, magic and found gold,
but of herself.
Strained confession of the burdened soul,
turned and plotted into place.

Spiders stared and listened as they worked,
drawn in against the will that wound.
Sirened as they sang.
Flies, even wasps and night moths,
were a distraction.

The Master

For three days and nights
a white dot spider clung
to an undistinguished place on the bedroom wall
and did not move.
Waiting for food, you would have said.
But he must have known by the second day
he had chosen poorly.
He would stay, he would have said,
by right of patience and possession.
This his home, his sacred space, his nation
to kill, if called upon, or die for.

The third day
when a moth crossed blindly within reach,
he let it pass.
Something neither of us expected or could explain
had happened here. He had learned,
in those unevented hours upon a wall,
what gifted yogis
in lives of abstinent meditation learn,
and he would not move.

The final day I found him.
Stiff beneath the world he'd made his own,
face up to the featureless white ceiling,
its burning bulb.
Mystic in the final stage of light.

Being Careful

I watched a small black dot, an ink spot spider,
cross the floor beside me.
It moved, not evenly,
but as a bird's head scanning its surrounding
turns, as gothic hands in steeple clocks
leap one minute to the next,
in quantum jumps, like protons.

And I wondered why, with all its fine swift legs,
it did not sweep more smoothly place to place.
And if the earth, observed from other space,
knowing there are wheres on every way
nothing, not even light, dares touch,
hurdles, vaults or skips as much,
and if these are leaps of faith.

Holding Its Place

A fly in the crease
between the pages of my book
rubbed two legs together,
in anticipation, surely,
of an absorbing read,
and waited.

I closed the book, slowly,
not to harm or threaten.
Just a clock, a calendar,
to say time passes, moves;
move on, but it did not move.

I gave it time, more time than fly
was ever given to escape,
but it held its place.
It had chosen, clearly,
to take its stand, be pressed here,
to be a word like other words almost.
To be, as we would, happened on.
Bid a reader, stopped by this strange shape,
touch what lit here once
and, ready, rubbing hands,
let the book close.

The Moth

Skimming the pantry shelf,
his motors were still running,
his wings slowing toward peace
when I brushed the moth away.

He became, all of him,
at that moment ash.
All his body entered it,
devoted what solidity it had
to the thin performance of mere stain.
It was as if,
scooping a finger to test for dust,
I had created it,
made of casual inquiry
small death.

My thumb's erasing
only spread it there
like a constable to shadows.
And I could feel its wealth,
this payment passed in darkness,
this loan more lasting than a life.

Hunger Artists

I remember the invasion of Japanese beetles,1944.
Burnished copper tanks swarming over leaves I couldn't see.

Looking back, it was a warning.
Our city streets like leaves.

But I was a child, taken with the glint of morning
on wings that fluttered golden when they moved.

How, close as kitten hairs, they scarcely touched,
respectful of another's need.

The reverential hum of their devouring.
The widow's sampler of the finest lace they left,

so fragile, spare and delicate I wondered how it held them,
so eerily exquisite, eaten through.

The Inner Life of Bees

What is a bee thinking
when it leaves a flower empty-winged, uncargoed?
Does it know the word "deceived"?
The feelings, disappointed, humbled?

Lifting, does it thrill, thrumming in its thorax,
to the petal wash of color,
hear in the hum of wings the bracing "Don't despair"?

Hauling pollen flower to flower,
does it know the rush of its beneficence?
Feel on its delicately antennaed crown
the unseen hand of hubris?
Cower from the beak of retribution?

Now, as it leaves with its sting its entrails,
like a flag in the conquered landscape of my arm,
does it weigh the costs and satisfactions of its power?
Does it feel in that vital, still-born moment
the fatal flush of martyred exultation?
Perceive in a blaze of fading light its chosenness,
born to suffer and redeem?

This honeyed menace
that pays for its passion with its life.

Two: Olive Trees

Olive Trees

I have been to the garden at Gethsemane.
I have seen the olive trees,
contorted, gnarled and twisted,
like lava stiffened in a windstorm.
I have experienced the wrenching fascination with their age,
their ugly beauty, what they have been through,
and the miracle that this was not

the merciless consequence of ineluctable decay—
Sequoias are as old, and magnificent.
Or of brutalizing weather—The climate here is temperate,
but for occasional aberrations almost kind.
Not even of what they were compelled to witness,
like a mother the rape or murder of her child.
The gouging urgency to warn, to rescue,
the deforming helplessness to move or speak.

No. It is in these trees to be as you see them.
In you to be in awe
of the indiscriminate generosities of design
and to crush their fruit for pleasure.

Amateur Gardening

The eleven boys,
ranged in age from ten to seventeen,
who crushed a neighbor's skull
with rakes and shovels,
pruning shears and hoes,
explained that they were city boys
untutored in the subtler points
of gardening.
They were all red thumbs.

Hitching a Ride

Every morning, I bring a folding chair
to the nearest highway,
sit on shoulders at the edge,
one leg across a knee, foot
just past the line where tended flowers
meet the roar of five-ton trucks,
as though I'm hitching,
which I am.

You'd never know it.
I'm staring at the summer
burst of berries on a bush,
the frantic flight of flies and moths
around them, the darting changes
of direction only godless aimlessness explains.

The idea,
to lean, head first, gently into traffic,
that a driver, noticing, will slow
and pull aside and take me on. Preferably
one who hasn't shaved in days,
who offers me a smoke or chaw
with a scarred four-fingered hand,
the stump of his index finger coarsely sewn
as though he trusted no one else to do it.
One whose crude blue skulls and crosses
are the only sleeve on his muscled arm
and I can see, when he opens them,
the still-wet blood of berries on his palms,
the look in his wild white eyes.

Strangers

Somewhere,
someone is digging a tunnel
whose port of egress
is a room in your home.

He is not a kind man,
well meaning
but quiet, patient
and determined.

When he emerges,
in your study, where you are reading,
in your kitchen, where you are eating,
in your bedroom while you sleep,

he will invite you into the tunnel
to testify it holds neither soap nor gloves
nor instruments for digging,
and he will show you clean hands.

He will become to you, to your surprise,
a person of interest,
and you will invite him
to join you in your study,

to share your lunch or dinner,
to lie down beside you and explain.
He will tell you nothing
you have not known or heard before.

But you will be drawn to his voice,
the exaggerated elasticity of his lips,
and you will remain,
but for an encouraging sigh or "I see," silent.

You will not,
and it will not occur to or surprise you
until long after,
ask or speak a word about the tunnel.

And because his hands are clean,
you will not mind if he touches you.
Not even your heart.

Old Faith

There is a bird, the elders say,
who, devouring man
one wretched morsel at a time,
devours his sins.

The pain to this bird is excruciating.
The poisoned skin and sinew,
mashed flesh and marrow,
gnaw inside him, but he does not stop.

He knows there are sins in your ribs
and ankles, sins in your tear ducts, cochlea
and calloused knees.
Sins of course—even you admit this—

in your teeth and tongue.
Sins long ago sequestered in your hair.
And you are going bald;
they are starting to reveal themselves.

People—some you say or thought
you loved—are staring.
The bird, with his small rasp tongue,
licks them off.

It is a mercy, but his feathers, because
he has done this for you, droop.
Each one, the weight of a small piano,
tears at him but will not come loose.

He bloats proportionally
to the age and magnitude of your sins.
He is not a Christian. The confessed
are not the smallest or most digestible.

Before he has reached your fingers,
where the worst are lodged
and lie in wait for him, in ambush,
he is the size of an apartment building.

The pain of the relentless pressure from within
is unbearable,
but the walls of his tormented body
will not give way.

He grows with goodness.
Larks and thrushes sing to him.
Tribesmen fall before him, worship him.
Sacred animals are sacrificed and burnt for him.

The smoke wafts toward him, soaks
into his tortured feathers,
and though he is not relieved by one iota,
he feels rewarded, paid.

At a time of his choosing—none knows when—
he throws up your remnants
that they may reassemble, harden
in the dirt before him, and begin again.

He is large of spirit.
You are given one more chance.
He remembers the anguish you have caused him.

Education

We leaned low across our wooden desks,
iron feet nailed three-toed to the floor
so we would not rock or steal them,

faces inches from the deep-carved
hearts and piercing arrows,
years, obscenities, and names

of those who leaned before us,
before the gouged walls blackened
with antiquity, as beaten leather will,

so that the whirlpool grain of treated ash
assumed the aura of an ancient binding,
precious, rare, impenetrable

but for the knowledge of a hidden history
that we, with pocket knives of fuming idleness,
became a part of.

Injustice

In Georgia, a seventeen-year-old boy, a robber,
shot a thirteen-month-old baby boy between the eyes
because his mother had no money.
Needless to say, this is intolerable.
Something must be done to prevent a recurrence.
There was undue haste here
and a reckless violation of procedure.
There should have been warning shots.
Two in the air and a crisply shouted "Halt!"
Then, if he didn't, one in the calf or knee,
preferably the knee.
And only then, if the baby still
wouldn't get out of the stroller,
the one that brought him down.
There are rules,
rules of engagement.
And something must be done
about a mother who has no money.

The Family

Annie Green,
mother of Roosevelt,
twenty-eight, of Georgia,
convicted of the kidnap,
rape, and murder
of a girl, eighteen,
watched his execution
by electric chair.
The papers said she
kept her calm.
A little tight about the lips,
but calm,
the boy a little tight about the thighs
when they strapped him in,
but calm.
God was with him
in his innocence, he said.
He hoped He was with others;
he had been reborn.
His father,
though he wished to be there,
had to wait outside.
They were afraid
he would not keep calm.
When it was over,
the doctor,
a little pale but calm,
emerged to tell him
mother and son were doing fine.

The News

The phone rang at 2 a.m.
Silence.
I could not sleep.
In the morning I saw them,
the familiar trio,
two in uniform,
inching up the walk.
Heard them knocking, softly,
advising me to sit,
asking someone to bring water.
Their faces fraught,
their voices trained and factual,
concerned.
They informed me, again,
of the death of someone far away
I'd never known.
I thanked them,
showed them out,
and tried to sleep.
The phone.

This Land

Every night the jackals come
to the prickly undergrowth beneath this porch,
pulled open from Mount Carmel
like a drawer with an unmatched sock.

Their cry is mournful, hopeless,
a wolf howl more like weeping.
I lean across the rail to see them,
but they are not for seeing.

Only a gleaming eye,
a spark yellow-flinted from the moon,
tells me it is not this land of soured milk, tart honey,
where cactus, gorse, and other bristling wild things thrive,
that wails.

A mother wandered
from the daily reinterment of her child
with the nightly news.
Her eye could ignite that bush,
could make it burn.

I Want to Know

I want to know they knew.
Of every raid and roundup in the square,
every train and transport,
every old man, infant, child and woman Jew
who died inside.
Inside the shit-choked cattle cars,
the less lucky who survived, inside.
Were there for the selection and experiments,
filling Jew eyes, mouths and throats with lye,
young Jew women's bellies with cement.
Knew of every death by suicide, typhus and starvation,
every pitside slaughter, gasing and cremation.
Saw the ashes on their rooves and tables, in their shoes.
And though they brushed them off for dinner,
listening calmly to the news,
and spilled them out before their Sunday
strolls to church, they knew.
I want to make *von jedem, der es wusste,**
my Jew.

     *of every one who knew

Left and Found

"There were people not
crying, not looking," she says, then she says
so much about us is unbearable.
("The Window," Sharon Olds)

They had left crying far behind.
Then, just after crying, longing,
love, regret, and the last one, wishing.
They were all here somewhere,
in the bare barracks, the stacked
straw beds where they were left,
last heard or heard from.
Some waking, more at night,
one in April, more in snow,
at roll call seven hours,
one more, perhaps the last,
in the ditch they peed and drained
their liquid feces and sometimes fell
or saw an old man tumble in,
and someone laughed.
Look, she says. Under this bed,
there's rage. Behind the door,
no forgiveness.
I'll take them home.

Three: Even As They Shudder

Shaking Off the Flies

I envy horses,
how they contract and shudder skin
to shake off flies
that disturb their grazing.

I try this with those I've loved
who will not let go.
Demeaning and ungrateful to call them flies.
But they have wings and sticky little legs
and many eyes.

Work, Bach's suites for cello unaccompanied,
you and all that live are leanings,
urgent brushes with the sensible,
like the nuzzling of mare and stallion in a field.
Sublimations of the skin's contractions
that do not stop with skin.

But I have watched these animals for hours.
The flies are patient, hovering, relentless.
The beautiful have learned somehow
to graze with dignity and grace,
even as they shudder.

The Unreal

Horses are not real.
They are cast in bronze or pewter,
hollowed out and set upon
a shelf somewhere they call the land.

Even when you call from fences,
cross with palm the flatted span
between their island eyes,
you know their sweat is polish,
their seeing obsidian or agate.

You have watched them
motionless for hours in the day's fluorescence,
broad tales lifted by a wind invisible as will
to brush those motish deaths, the flies.

When you blink, their skin shell twitches
like a snake in preparation
or a time of day.
If they were real,
you would find translucent husks discarded,

as when they dipped their heads,
the arc would be other than the earth's
or the bow light bends
across the fondest inferences
among the stars.

On the Generosity of Evolution

Flies stroll, window-shop, or doze on ceilings,
enabled by the sticky tips of setae in their pulvilli.
I'm pleased for their sake evolution thought of this,
sensed its service to survival,
though I'm not sure why.

Who is after them in here?
Frogs with their foot-long party-favor tongues
feed in swamps and ponds
where a ceiling's rare as size twelve,
triple E width fly feet or a feathered moon.
Likewise birds in gardens, branches, fields
where the only overhead is sky.

Perhaps they used it first
for gluing needles head to point
that camels and the rich,
turned back bloody at the eye, might climb
and discovered this by chance.

You've seen children hanging upside down
from playground bars, heads thrown back,
hair like mountain cataracts in air, and laughing.
Giddy Adams waking to a world they've never seen
and won't let go.

And you, though fearful, calling, shutting eyes,
love them so for holding on,
for loving earth, as you do, turned this way,
you forget the sticky feet of flies.
Grateful evolution thought you'd need this,
plucked you out for just this gift, this moment,
though nothing in this life will tell you why.

Preserved

Have you ever crushed a firefly?
Underfoot and ground your heel
the way we once crushed beetles, ants?
Smeared its yellow light like the time-lapse passage
of a night train in cement?
Movement stilled, like time,
a moment life was light.

I believe things last, preserved somewhere,
if we could find them. Every spoken word in air.
Every gasp of grateful thrill you thought unheard
when one you knew would not, comes back.
What light illumines, gathers in,
like sand when the wave rolls out.
Part of ocean.
Crouched in light and waiting.

It was in a park when I was eight or nine.
The tree a tuning orchestra of blinking light
that found one note.
That snapped me startled,
caught that child, that stare,
the moment that would not return,
and kept it.

If I crushed a firefly, it would be for this.
The chance, a thousand generations on,
that otherworldly A of tuning horns and viols here,
the boy who saw.
I'd kneel beside it on the walk,
touch this stain I feel now sink beneath my skin,
beg forgiveness, bless it.

The Balance

This rotting raw wood
one-room cabin on my land
leans on logs
crosshatched on broken slabs of slate
stacked like griddle cakes on a tilted table.

Groans, since these alone won't hold,
against a tree whose bark
weeps in torrents with the strain,
root-limbs lifted to their knees
like a body, dripping, craned
from the deep silt bottom of a lake.

A boulder, half unearthed, the last defense,
stakes its weight, our faith, against the fall.
And yet the mice and garden snakes,
the cabin's only summer residents,
drawn together to one side
by the mournful call of owls one night,
might be all the downhill slope of nature asks
to tip it.

Against Gravity

Every autumn
the saffron, brown and scarlet sheddings
of the maple trees that lined our streets
swayed and spiraled, danced digressive currents down,
moments almost rising as they fell.

Like the woman leaping
from the highest window in the burning tower—
who spread her red skirt wide,
as though she curtseyed,
then her naked arms, turning face
and breasts up to the sky,
and called—it wasn't meant for us,
but we could hear her: Look!

The Immigrants

When the sun is low,
the way of light that strikes the sea
is of another world, of soul,
or takes us.

It is corrugated silver.
Hard, not water.
You needn't be a god
to walk it; it will hold you up.

The danger is from crowds,
the bearded, winged and
white-robed figures teeming toward you
from the other side.

They have seen the jeweled sand,
the dark earth and dew-specked
grass behind it. They have seen trees
trying desperately to hold their leaves.

They have seen leaves fall,
the fires burnt orange, red,
and smelled in the blackened smoke their dying.
They will not be stopped.

The conversion has begun already.
You can see it in their widened eyes,
their thickened legs and feet,
their sweat.

The polite will step aside to let you pass.
The rude, impatient, will force you from the path
or walk right through you.
The best will plead with you to show them.

God's Exhaustion

It's after Yom Kippur, and God is resting.
Forgiveness exhausts him.
Learning how many ways we've sinned exhausts him.
Watching hungry men and women pound their hearts
exhausts him. Seeing some slip broken bits of bread
from pockets to their mouths, as though
they tighten teeth, exhausts him.
Hearing them exalt and praise his might,
dazzling in their ignorance, depresses him.

How will he measure up to such assumptions?
What labors will be set before him? What proofs required?
The very thought exhausts him.
Listening to their tearful cries of gratitude
for favors he cannot remember tires him.
So many fall upon their knees and name them,
he wonders, worries that his memory, prodigious once,
absolute when there were only seven days, is failing.
The fear exhausts him.

Learning how they dread his anger,
tremble at a jealous rage they do not provoke
weighs him down.
That they cower at one whose mercy's boundless,
so they say, bewilders him.
Truly, when they slaughter, rape, burn towns,
run rivers with each other's blood and tie him to their crimes,
he is irked, annoyed.
But jealous anger? Rage?

That only for the rolling waves of oceans.
The blink and blaze and burning out of stars.
The alarming autumn turn of leaves
to scarlet, sunset orange, gold.

The summer flash of northern lights
that give sky passion, hunger, breath, the urge to move.
Excited children thronging in the street
who will not heed the call to come inside
for reasons no better than the dark.

The Unnamed

(to Paul and Miriam on the birth of their son)

Imagine a swaddled newborn suspended among stars,
lighting a path through the sea,
as though the Jews were heading out again,
this time at night, and called for torches.
It looks as much like a half moon
as anything I can think of,
and though we can't stop chattering,
the lakes and hills are silent in its presence.

Whoever we are, we're all Jews here,
looking for the way home,
and who's to say this isn't
the soft palimpsest of light we're looking for?
I'm not saying you should call him Moon.
But if you approach it as he did,
pointing, looking up, mouth a little open
in small amazement, you won't miss.
Like the sun, as it moves on,
sending back
all the shine curves and distances can take
to hint at origins,
identify a shape,
engrave with brightness what is there,
as with a name.

Inflated Moon

I'm bowled over when the moon,
lower than it should be, is bigger than you've ever seen it.
Must have grown over day somehow
large as earth, at least, maybe Saturn
and, ready, hangs its funhouse mirror face
over the tree and rooftops like the superhero's clownish nemesis,
back for another fiendish try.

While you were brushing teeth, downing toast and oatmeal,
working on a busted pipe or manuscript,
eyeing her who shouldn't look and dress like that
strolling past your desk or manhole,
you had no idea the moon was crouching
behind an arras of late summer light, growing,
pumping itself up like an air mattress,
mumbling some unpronounceable twenty-letter word
backwards that inflates it ten times its normal size, ready for night.

Makes you realize, the one you love and thought loved you,
the one whose middle, full and quarter name is love,
the moon, for heaven's sake, can turn on you,
pull the ocean over a million rooves and drown us all.
Or if not, just hang there,
flashing its outsized anguished grimace
as though not sweetness, strength,
but all earth's accumulated insult, pain
has crusted to a cratered ball about to barrel
through the flimsy line of half-lit high-rise buildings,
flattening every stiff and moving thing
to where you're sitting in your parked car, shaking, gawking.

And how magnificent fear—
if you can just get hold of it,
if you're blessed with a little time, a life,
to stare at death and look away—can be.

The Greater Miracle

We met in the garden of a mutual friend.
Someone's birthday or anniversary, I think.
But I remember only
that she was bright, vivacious, glowing.
We spoke, congenially, about a dozen things—
weather, movies, the yellow tulips, politics
and where they lived—and laughed,
because that's where ease and pleasure go
when they come this far.

"How many children?"
"One," she said.
"Our daughter disappeared
somewhere in Brazil five years ago.
Perhaps you read or heard about it then.
It was in the news.
She's still 18 for us.
How old are yours?"

And I knew all I needed to
of God, the human and belief.
How she could have born the child in purity,
how he walked on water, raised the dead,
how the sun froze on order in the sky
to let the loaves and fishes cool,
and how the split sea held our people in parentheses
the story needed to go on.

Like the first few days:
the light and darkness,
gathered waters, grass,
the trees that in their seasons bring forth fruit,
living things that fly and swim
and creep or lumber on the land.

Warm-ups for the main event,
the one we read and heard about
and crawled upon the land to see.
The miracle in the garden, it was called.
The one who swallows death
and hurls up life.

What Holds

A branch of the tree beside my house,
split with age or lightning in a storm,
holds by a clean thin strip of perfect underskin
that shines.

The tree is bare, fleshless finger-crooked
as dead trees are.
Only the hanging branch says leaves,
broken at the neck by too much life,
as hung men are.

And yet, how clean and fresh what holds
behind each limb, each length of flesh,
loved thing, inside us.

The cry as body tears, at loss,
wet, white, terrible and new
as the cry of birth.

Four: Lapped Water

Old Wind

The wind is getting old.
It lurches forward, stumbles,
rocks and totters on its heels,
then rests on a garden wall or bench
to catch its breath.
Not that it's going anywhere.
Just out for its recommended daily airing,
though no one walks beside it,
lends a caring arm to steady it,
or chatters on a cell phone when it sleeps.

I remember how it whistled when it strode or sprang.
How it mimed the whine of sirens
or ran beside and rubbernecked to see
who they'd taken off this time,
paused a moment, there but for the grace,
then raced ahead or peeled away,
sang through unlit alleys unafraid.

Remember how he scooped
light scraps and tabloid pages from the street,
juggled leaves in streaming banners overhead.
How, so taken with the red and gold,
the rustle of applause
when he loosened, shook them free,
he wasn't thinking when they're gone
how cold he'd be, and how, all night sometimes,
through cracks where sliding doors are an inch awake,
like a small child calling to those inside, he'd cry.

Duel

When I lift myself from bed at dawn
to meet my walk,
pacing out, like a purblind duelist,
a few more steps for life,

young runners lap me
like stagnant waiting water
in a bowl.

She took everything in the room with her
when she went

A friend has taken her life.
By the time of its taking
it was small and light, compacted,
so although she could not walk,
she believed it would be easy to carry.

Sleepspeech

I sleep this speech,
dream into the small boat of thing and space
the current takes.

Hung branches brush,
half wake me
if I sweep too close.

Too far from driftwood, bone hands
that spin in place like an old man's questions,
thoughts, that can't let go, move on.

Dragonflies that break so sharply, often,
you'd think they're frightened at the sight of
absence here of anything to turn them.

The muffled thud that almost wakes me
when a bottle with a folded message knocks,
like someone lost at midnight at the bow.

Closing

There is a kind of cloud
that smears the sky, erases it.
As though something
has changed its mind,
would start again
or, beaten, walk away.

Like soaped white windows
when a store that prospered once—
perfect mannequins, he and she,
in stiff but "Here-am-I-and-here's-my-lover" poses,
changing dress to match the seasons—
goes out of business or has moved.

Usually, there's a Clearance Sale before,
when he and she, in separate rooms,
smile like mannequins at buyers,
lie "We've lost our lease
but know you'll love this reading lamp, this bed."

The sky? There
it's often without warning.
An early death or accident,
infidelity, protracted mourning, grief,
or just the slow erosion of belief.

Two Stories

Their father's gone, galloped off
to darkness, gone.
The girls write stories.

In the younger's tale, she's ten;
the boy is terrified his stallion
will collapse beneath him in mid-ride,

its legs folding like lobster claws,
his body pitched like tiles
from an Alpine roof.

The boy is anxious, frightened.
His stomach bubbles tar
hardening at his chest and feet.

His mother reassures him.
She speaks of stars, the faithful flowering
in the stubborn east, and the wall of China.

He is unconsoled but grateful.
At night he dreams of pillars
pressed against and broken

by a blinded Samson in the swirling robes of God.
His mother sleeps beside him,
her palm at his ribs.

In the elder's tale, she's twelve;
the mother works long hours.
She is never home, a stranger,

and they are surprised
and a little frightened
that she owns a key.

The father works only
when the daughters are at school.
He is her uniform, her book bag.

When she opens it, he is her ruler, her compass,
her soft reliable eraser,
though she hates how he withers when he cleans.

She has a friend whose mother
is a daily meal for cancer.
She reassures him.

She speaks of clouds in a high blue wind,
of the blooming change of color
in bright leaves,

though if it comes to that, she says,
he will share their home.
At night she dreams she is a stallion.

The Visitor, A Modern Fable

One in every two, almost, will suffer it,
and though we've announced a war,
the aliens swarm in, the terror blooms.
Pollution of the air and body summon it,
but it needs no call.
Demonic Goldilocks, it visits uninvited,
knows the way through bolted doors and windows,
feeds and fattens on the fare and never sleeps,
with fierce eye open, naps.

It is enough to own a cottage in the woods.
Or town or city.
To let the porridge cool. And walk.
Is this not us, this fabled setting out and wandering,
this cunning spread of self and seed across the land,
conquest at the end, expansion?
These are the sky god's faithful children,
the fruit and multiplicity he ordered
heeded deep within. They are gathered early
to his love, his longing.

Soon, hungry for their porridge,
sweetly cool and edible by now,
the strolling bears return.
The little girl with the swollen belly does not flee.
She shows them in the mirror the purchased deed.
They will live, the bears and growing golden girl,
in this crowded home together.
Not always happily.
Not forever.
Managing with this new arrangement.
For a while.

Actually

he didn't want the child.
What would he have done with her,
there in the feral woods, alone?
What did he know of diapers,
bottle feedings, what to do
if she woke him,
crying in the night and would not stop?

It was when he saw the servant
on the hill that he lit the fire,
danced and sang aloud and sang again.

How else would he have been blessed
to see her even those three days?
Watch her face refashion hope
to desperation, fear,
then leap, as then, to joy
like flax to gold?

Know a second time
her need for what he knew?
Hear the song, on those red lips,
the strange, surprising beauty of his name.

Island

An island in the middle of a thoroughfare.
There are flowers here, daffodils and petunias.
Whatever lasts, whatever like old men,
in thick brown coats of our pollution, will not die.
Also a fence, repainted every year or two
to say, like the sun giving way,
like an aging woman's face and hair,
not only leaving and coming back,
that color matters.

And on the fence a small man leans
like a rancher timing his racehorse,
though he is old, his bunched face
furrowed like a Chinese dog, his camel coat
miles and generations out of season.
This is summer, and he a month
no year has yet made room for.

He is so small, he peers between
at what rides by.
The years and this intensity compress him.
To the vehicles that pass,
he is a bale of metal on a mound of parts.
Here and there, the camel's hairs admit
the browner rust of understanding;
where he was splashed, perhaps
when the Allies hit Bataan
or the rain, with a relentlessness
uncommon even for the rain, inscribed its name.

They say he came before the island and first seeds.
Nothing grows in his shadow,
his coat a bell that muffles sound, his body
a thick and speechless cast iron tongue,
plumb line to the molten center of all things.

They say the fence is there to keep him back,
that only traffic and the lights, not he,
will slow you down.
If you look aside, you will see nape hairs like grass
in cold wind rising that he does not.

What's Played

Softball, soccer, the saxophone too loud next door at 6 a.m.,
a cello eerily at midnight.
Poker for more money than he had.
She warned him not to, but he played
on her weakness for his folly, and she gave in.
The dogs and ponies, Keeno. The phonograph
and CD player, Schubert's Death and the Maiden.
Old radio broadcasts: Fred Allen, The Answer Man,
Jack Armstrong, Inner Sanctum and The Quiz Kids
on a tape deck. You're almost in tears.
Chess with your son, letting him win, fattening his ego
till he's good enough to beat you and you beg off,
saying you're tired, the weather's good, and he should be outside
playing, getting fresh air and exercise.
Moonlight with water, a glittering path
as from another world or life—
studded for angels or the dead, who miss it here—
or to it.
Wind with birch leaves, like baby hands or castanets,
through the crack in the sliding glass door against the sea,
so it sounds like sirens, jackals, a terrible loneliness,
an Arab mother grieving.
Possum, like Ali on the ropes, waiting his turn.
Dead, like the Ukranian Jew under layers of bodies
in the pit at Babi Yar, gagging on blood, praying for dark.
The Ten Commandments at the Roosevelt Theater
where the Filippino yo yo champ does loop the loop
and walk the dog to your amazement.
An old widow, sending her savings to the man who sounded
so earnest and believable, for a sucker.
A stricken teenager by a married man who swears he'll marry her,
for a sucker.

The prettiest coed at the reading, maybe literally this time,
for a sucker.
Doctor with the little girl next door. Yours first.
Hide and Seek, Giant Steps, Cops and Robbers,
Three Steps Off to Germany.
Taps at Flanders, Arlington and Normandy,
for the dead.

Five: Stone/Glass

Summer Night

When we sat out on the front porch at 2 a.m.,
too hot, even with a window fan, to sleep inside,
I felt blessed.

We were all there.
Mother and father, seen as husband, wife,
man and woman on occasion, maybe.
Never as now.

Two sons, known once or twice as brothers.
This was once.

Even the moon disturbed the stillness
of the shadow houses, other porches, trees,
the clouds their silence.

No one spoke.

All faces seemed relaxed, relieved.
Rescued from the same oppressive, stifling thing
that for this hour, these minutes, wasn't us.

No Planet

They have discovered
a new celestial body
in the neighborhood of Pluto,
which is to say
less than a million miles away.
No planet, they suspect,
it is merely asteroids
twining one another
with possessive love,
flaring gossip in each other's ears
about the infidelity of moons,
the spurning coldness of a once-warm star.
Huddling tightly, like a family,
in the dark.

Dance Night

Asbury Park, late 40s, on the Jersey shore.
New Lafayette Hotel, a treat two weeks each summer,
my mother, my brother and I.
My father, the stuttering salesman—what a choice of occupation!—
who worked when he summoned up the nerve,
sank more often in his fraying easy chair behind the news,
joined us weekends only.
As though the headlines called him home, he couldn't stay.

I remember one. Dance contest night,
and they were out there on the dance floor,
my mother and her man,
closer, more accordant than I'd ever seen them.
He leading as he'd never done,
she for the first time willing, whirling and aglow.
Fred and Ginger, so familiar, smooth and easy,
they must have done this, lived this, called it life
before the real one tapped him on the shoulder,
stepped between them, danced her off.

People stood and whistled, cheered.
Me too, throat-and-stomach-choked, in tears,
and they won, hands down, thumbs up.
The prize a bottle of champagne they still,
to the day he left, years later,
hadn't touched.

Electric

I loved the flash and crack of sparks above the trolley,
in wires their wasp antenna touched.
Like fingers to a standing lamp or unsuspecting hand
when we rubbed the deep pile rugs of childhood
with Aladdin feet and learned we were electric,
felt the crackling voltage of connection.

It had its price. The shock,
as of surprise each time, that drove us back;
but, small experimenting gods, we could not stop.
Charged, like Him, with lonely innocence,
we did not dream how soon
they'd roll the lawns and gardens up.
How touch would dumbly dim toward touch.
How unwittingly we'd prepare ourselves for love.

The Mission

I saw once
the dark sun settle in the middle of the sea.
Surrounded.
I expected
a pandemonium of hissing,
as of a thousand serpents
foiled by Eve's indifference,
wind in the tree's dead leaves
when she bit through.
This and a whirlpool galaxy of waves
hurtling from the eye to try again.

But the sea was not unsettled,
not consumed.
The golden path, shadow-barred
through clouds like ladder rungs,
lay quiet in blue grass,
and I removed my shoes,
stepped back and watched the half disc
slowly feed itself to waves,
assign no mission
but to feel the blooded glory
on the way to dark
like the crush of early love
around the heart.

Physics 101

My favorite experiment in Physics class
was the one with the candle in a closed tin can.
When the flame sucks all its oxygen, the can implodes,
collapses, as though the hand of the Incredible Hulk
or Adam Smith—that was Economics—crushed it.

Another I liked, a small lead weight set gently
in a bowl of water, proved what we'd all learn later:
If an object displaces more
than its own weight or density, it sinks.

Do you see what I'm up to, where I'm going?
If not, try the Law of Fall, which holds:
The distance traveled by a body in free fall
(we'll call it flight)
is in proportion to the square of the fall's duration.
The longer it takes to fall, in other words—
or, with a slight adjustment of the universe,
to begin its fall—the greater its distance
from the place it left.
Also, the greater its velocity as it speeds away,
unless it is slowed, deflected, or abruptly stopped
by something it encounters in its path.

This is known as the principle of inertia,
but it is poorly named.
Like all the elementary laws of physics,
it has little to do with inertia.
More with the death of an illusion,
with asphyxiation, imbalance and the end of love.

Coincidence

"I apologize to coincidence for calling it necessity"
("Under a Certain Little Star," Wisława Szymborska)

Like seeing you walk towards me on stiletto heels
   in that tight black boat-neck sweater, rocking
   those astonishing blue-green eyes,
having no idea where you'd be at just that moment
   had I not learned, stumbling on the steadfast pattern
   of your whereabouts and movements over the past
   five weeks, six days, that this was always where you
   were at just this time.

Like saying, miraculously, just the right four words
   by way of hopeful but embarrassed introduction,
having no idea what you'd find appealing, childish
   or offensive. Trusting entirely to intuition, luck
   and the coincidental overhearing of nineteen introductions
   by assorted eager strangers over the past two months,
   nine days—eighteen failed, one unsettling
   but instructively successful.

Like knowing where to take you that fortuitous first evening,
knowing nothing of your taste in music or your dining
   preferences but what I'd learned from thirty-seven friends,
   acquaintances and relatives who, for reasons I cannot
   explain, even to this day, gave me just that information
   when I interviewed them for a survey about the leisure
   occupations of young women of a certain class I happened
   to be conducting at the time.

Like knowing, somehow, eight years later you'd be leaving,
   when you said, excitedly, you'd met, by odd coincidence,
   precisely where we'd met eight years before, a stranger
   who seemed to know you.

Cleaving

To cleave.
To adhere or cling, remain faithful to,
especially in resistance to a force that draws away.
Also to split or divide,
as by a cutting blow, especially
along a natural line of division,
like the grain of wood.

Where has this word been?
In the flower beds, perhaps,
concealed among the lilacs and nasturtiums.
Watching through a window—
now the bedroom,
now the living room or study.
Observing, researching us unnoticed,
as for a project or assignment.
Learning more than a word
or anyone should know.
Or we, in a thousand words,
in all this cleaving silence, could have said.

Mainlining Clouds

When there are no clouds,
there's nothing worth saying about the sky
but that it's speechless.

It's the table turned over in the storm,
legs stiff in air like road kill,
that wakes us, gets us talking.

Shows how, when the sheriff wind
that gave the drunken clouds till noon subsides,
sea, blue flat, plays sky
and one dead thing is like another.

Take you, take me, hunched in corners,
rubber tubing knotted at the crook,
mainlining clouds.

Look. The porch chair blasted to its knees,
leaning on its elbows, forehead touching tile.
Praying to its thundering, shrouded-
in-the-whirlwind god to save us.

Red Sea

They can tell
by the fitting crookedness of coasts
the continents broke apart a while ago
and drifted.

Blind, I run my hand
along the contours of my body,
front and side,
fingering the Braille of separation,
remember yours.
But we were always water,
never land; I find no sign.

I tell myself
it was an act of God
to let a nation through.
Nothing less will do.

Talking Trailer

Every Tuesday, driving my son to kindergarten,
the only day he still was mine,
we'd pass a parked RV,
a once-white, perhaps abandoned hookup
that never moved.
One morning, in a soft affectionate falsetto,
it began to speak.
To greet my son with pleasure,
with unabashed, untempered joy
at seeing him pass by.
As if it stirred its static metal heart to see him.

Not that it was lonely,
never left its place before that square stone house,
though it seemed almost deflated there, sunk in.
More that it had much to tell each morning,
what it had seen and done the day before.
What country roads it traveled,
what beaches, wooded hills and meadows it had waved to.
What tree-lined lanes, where leaves meeting overhead
would separate sometimes to let in light,
and how it blazed.
What other vehicles and riders stopped to chat
and what they'd said.

What excited it to high-pitched, uncanny human speech
was a child it thought might listen,
even answer questions to sate its curiosity,
speak shyly, a little hesitantly at first,
then with luck more openly of where he'd been,
what he'd seen and done since they last met,

long after we were out of range, the trailer far behind,
and no one there but us on the way to school.

Drinking the Sea

(a lullabye for Etai)

When he couldn't sleep,
I'd press his tiny body to my chest,
set his teacup chin in my shoulder's rest
that I might be his violin
and sing him up and down the corridor
between his bedroom and our own.
Rockabye Baby a hundred
dying-toward-a-whisper times until he slept.

I was forty-four, my spine a twisted
olive branch that proposed no peace.
And within minutes, where the bough
for the thirty-seventh time gives way,
I'd feel my own. Feel it curtsy, bow,
swing its vertebrae like a white-plumed hat
and step aside for anguish, wide as any pavement,
striding through.

No shifting of his six apples and a grapefruit weight,
no Tarot, leaf, or palm-read realignment
with the moons of Saturn, piety or stars
would detain it with a friendly conversation,
block its way.
Only the glassy smoothness of his skin,
the world these foundling months lends out,
lays at our doorstep, sparkling
its flat sandpaper smile when we take it in.
This and the swooning scent of newness I sucked in,
deep as the Chinese brother in the tale
who could drink in a single draught the sea.

He calls sometimes, from another continent,
for help with something costly, broken,
or in his love life not quite right.

It isn't easy. He's a little heavier now, my size,
but though he wears a three-months beard
and sweats a little on the treadmill
or weeding with his woman in their yard,
I lift him still, set his satin-smooth sweet chin
where throat and shoulder meet to let him in
and drink the sea to reach him.

The Words She Knew

When my widowed aunt was eighty,
she met a man she'd loved at twenty,
before she met the man she'd never love.
"It hasn't changed," she said.
"It feels the same," and blushed.
He kissed her sweetly at the door,
but never called again.
He had money, hair, and didn't devour small children.
Younger widows called and stammered when he spoke,
and he was gone.
"It doesn't change," she said.
"It feels the same," and wept.

Weeks later, something broke in her heart and brain
and leaked near death.
She could drag her limbs and speak,
but couldn't remember the commonest words.
When the hospital nurse,
shapely, blonde and engaged to a diamond,
showed her a picture of a chair,
and my aunt said "chair,"
the fiancée fawned and gurgled.
"Wonderful!" she squealed. "That's wonderful!
Yes, chair."
The widow fixed her from the corner
of her eighty years,
thirty with a man she never loved, the rest without,
and scowled.
"Wonderful," she grumbled.
"I can recognize a chair."

She stumbled over key and window,
umbrella, porcupine and iron, but never love.

When I said I loved her,
"It feels the same," she said. "It never goes away,"
and stared beyond me.
On her way to the bathroom,
in nothing but her loose green gown
the night before the last,
she peed on the floor.
She didn't say she couldn't help it,
and those were words she knew.

The Lesson

When my cat brought a bird, half eaten,
and dropped it at my feet,
I sat it down for a discussion
on the sofa, which is usually forbidden.
I spoke calmly, but firmly,
in simple language I assumed it would understand,
in homilies and parables that exemplified,
about respect for life, however humble,
the Sixth Commandment,
about doing unto others and doing not.
About the beautiful; and it seemed,
though chastened, grateful.

When my cat next day
brought a rat it had half devoured
and dropped it at my feet,
I was appalled and turned away.
Inviting me to the field,
where I rarely go, for a discussion,
it sat beside me where the grass had worn away
and spoke, with the calm assurance knows,
in language it assumed I would understand,
about motive and intent,
about identity and limit,
what can and cannot be learned.
About acceptance, with gratitude and grace,
of what we're given.

Stone/Glass

Where the water stops
I found a stone like sea-green glass,
or glass like a pale translucent stone,
I could not tell.

Something from the world-deep belly of beginning,
rocked and delivered by the waves,
or something lime-kilned, molded, made.
Something so like love, the lasting agony of grief,
I could not tell.

Acknowledgments

Some of these poems have been published in the following journals:

Alpeiron Review: "Old Faith"
Anthropoid: "This Land," "Hunger Artists"
Backstreet: "Injustice," "The Greater Miracle"
Birchbrook: "The Balance"
Blueline: "Learning about Rain"
Cactus Heart: "The Visitor: A Modern Fable"
California Quarterly: "Stories"
Cider Press Review: "The Unnamed"
Common Ground: "Drinking the Sea"
Convergence: "On the Generosity of Evolution"
Darkling: "Amateur Gardening"
Deronda Review: "Cleaving," "Coincidence"
Hidden Oak: "No Planet"
Main Street Rag: "Hitching a Ride"
Nassau Review: "Island"
Rattle: "She took everything in the room with her when she went"
Seventh Quarry: "The Unused" (retitled here "What Holds")
Slipstream: "Physics 101"
Spillway: "The Mission"
Straylight: "Inflated Moon"
The Quarterly: "The Family," "The Moth"
The Stray Branch: "Strangers"

The following poems appeared in earlier collections by the author
published by Ginninderra Press (Adelaide, Australia):

Being Them All (2005): "The Moth"
Some Can (2009): "The Family," "Two Stories," "The Visitor"
Last Things and After (2011): "The Mission"

About FutureCycle Press

FutureCycle Press is dedicated to publishing lasting English-language poetry books, chapbooks, and anthologies in both print-on-demand and Kindle ebook formats. Founded in 2007 by long-time independent editor/publishers and partners Diane Kistner and Robert S. King, the press incorporated as a nonprofit in 2012. A number of our editors are distinguished poets and writers in their own right, and we have been actively involved in the small press movement going back to the early seventies.

The FutureCycle Poetry Book Prize and honorarium is awarded annually for the best full-length volume of poetry we publish in a calendar year. Introduced in 2013, our Good Works projects are anthologies devoted to issues of universal significance, with all proceeds donated to a related worthy cause. Our Selected Poems series highlights contemporary poets with a substantial body of work to their credit; with this series we strive to resurrect work that has had limited distribution and is now out of print.

We are dedicated to giving all of the authors we publish the care their work deserves, making our catalog of titles the most diverse and distinguished it can be, and paying forward any earnings to fund more great books.

We've learned a few things about independent publishing over the years. We've also evolved a unique, resilient publishing model that allows us to focus mainly on vetting and preserving for posterity poetry collections of exceptional quality without becoming overwhelmed with bookkeeping and mailing, fundraising activities, or taxing editorial and production "bubbles." To find out more about what we are doing, come see us at www.futurecycle.org.

The FutureCycle Poetry Book Prize

All full-length volumes of poetry published by FutureCycle Press in a given calendar year are considered for the annual FutureCycle Poetry Book Prize. This allows us to consider each submission on its own merits, outside of the context of a contest. Too, the judges see the finished book, which will have benefitted from the beautiful book design and strong editorial gloss we are famous for.

The book ranked the best in judging is announced as the prize-winner in the subsequent year. There is no fixed monetary award; instead, the winning poet receives an honorarium of 20% of the total net royalties from all poetry books and chapbooks the press sold online in the year the winning book was published. The winner is also accorded the honor of being on the panel of judges for the next year's competition; all judges receive copies of all contending books to keep for their personal library.